AI Tax Forecasting & Withholding Optimization

How to Avoid Owing Money at Tax Time

By Joe Correa

Published by Live Stronger Faster

This book is for educational and informational purposes only. The author and publisher are not engaged in rendering legal, financial, tax, or other professional advice. Readers should consult a qualified professional before making any financial decisions.

First Edition

Table of Contents

Introduction

Most people believe tax problems happen in April, but in reality, tax problems are created every single day throughout the year. Every paycheck, every side hustle payment, every investment trade, every withdrawal, and every expense silently reshapes what you will owe or be refunded months later. By the time most taxpayers see their return, the outcome is already locked in. The surprise bill, the smaller-than-expected refund, or the frustrating penalty is not caused by something that happened in April—it is caused by the lack of forecasting and optimization that should have been happening all year long. This is exactly where artificial intelligence changes the rules of the tax system forever. Instead of guessing, hoping, or waiting, AI now allows individuals to see the future of their taxes in real time and make adjustments before damage occurs.

For decades, tax withholding has been one of the most misunderstood parts of personal finance. People fill out a W-4 when they start a job, check a few boxes, and then never think about it again, even as their income, family situation, side income, deductions, and investments change. The IRS then quietly withholds too much or too little from every paycheck, often without the taxpayer realizing it. Too much withholding means you gave the government an interest-free loan all year. Too little means penalties, stress, and scrambling to come up with money at filing time. Traditional tax software can only tell you what already happened, but artificial intelligence can tell you what is about to happen—and how to fix it before it does.

AI tax forecasting is the ability of advanced algorithms to analyze your current income, past tax history, deductions, credits, investments, and financial behavior, then project forward what your tax liability will be months into the future. This is not a rough estimate or a simple calculator. Modern AI models can simulate thousands of tax scenarios in seconds, factoring in changes to income, inflation, IRS rule updates, and even potential life events. Instead of asking "How much did I owe last year?", AI asks "How much will I owe if I keep doing what I am doing right now?" and then gives you precise levers to change the outcome. This shifts taxation from a reactive process to a proactive financial strategy.

One of the most powerful uses of AI in tax forecasting is withholding optimization. This means continuously adjusting how much tax is taken out of your paychecks or estimated payments so that you end the year as close to zero as possible—without penalties and without overpaying. In a perfect system, you would owe nothing and be owed nothing, keeping your money in your own hands all year long. AI systems can monitor income changes, bonuses, overtime, commissions, freelance income, rental profits, crypto gains, and investment income in real time and instantly recommend changes to withholding or estimated tax payments. Instead of guessing on a W-4 once a year, you can now run a living, breathing tax strategy that updates automatically as your financial life evolves.

This matters more than ever because modern income is no longer simple. Many people earn from multiple jobs, side hustles, gig work, online businesses, rental properties, dividends, crypto trading, and retirement withdrawals—all at the same time. Each income stream is taxed differently, and each affects your marginal tax rate. A small increase in income can push you into a higher bracket, trigger phase-outs of credits, or cause you to under-withhold without realizing it. AI excels at handling this complexity because it does not think in single streams—it thinks in systems. It sees how everything interacts, then calculates how much tax should be withheld today to avoid pain tomorrow.

AI also solves one of the biggest psychological problems in taxes: uncertainty. When people do not know what they will owe, they feel anxiety all year long. They either avoid looking or overpay just to feel safe. With AI forecasting, you can open a dashboard and see a running estimate of your tax position—how much you are projected to owe or be refunded if nothing changes, and how that changes when income goes up, expenses increase, or deductions are added. This clarity allows you to make intelligent decisions about taking on more work, making investments, or spending money because you can see the tax impact before you act.

Another revolutionary benefit of AI tax forecasting is scenario modeling. You can ask questions like, "What happens to my taxes if I sell this stock?" "What if I take on a new freelance client?" "What if I convert to a Roth IRA?" or "What if I buy a rental property?" The AI can instantly simulate the tax consequences of each move across the entire year and beyond. This allows you to plan income and timing in a way that minimizes taxes legally and strategically. Instead of being surprised by tax bills, you are designing them in advance.

For families, withholding optimization becomes even more powerful. Changes in dependents, child tax credits, education expenses, health insurance, and retirement contributions all affect how much tax should be withheld. AI systems can monitor these changes and adjust recommendations accordingly. If a child is born, if a student loan is paid off, or if healthcare costs spike, the AI updates the forecast instantly. This creates a dynamic, living tax plan that evolves alongside your life. This book will show you how AI-powered tax forecasting tools work, how they connect to your income sources and financial accounts, and how they calculate your future tax position. You will learn how AI models interpret tax brackets, credits, deductions, and IRS rules to produce real-time projections that are far more accurate than traditional calculators. You will also learn how to translate those projections into actionable steps—updating W-4 forms, adjusting estimated payments, changing savings and investment strategies, and timing income in smarter ways.

You will also discover how AI helps protect you from penalties and underpayment traps. Many taxpayers are unaware that the IRS requires certain minimum payments throughout the year, not just in April. AI systems track these thresholds automatically and warn you when you are approaching risk. They can even generate reminders, payment schedules, and optimized contribution plans so you stay compliant while still minimizing what you give up.

AI tax forecasting is not just about avoiding bad surprises—it is about maximizing opportunity. When you know your future tax position, you can deploy your money more intelligently. You can invest, save, spend, or reinvest with confidence, knowing that your tax obligations are already accounted for. This turns taxes from a hidden threat into a visible, manageable part of your wealth strategy. In the chapters that follow, you will learn how to build a real-time tax forecast using AI, how to optimize your withholding across multiple income sources, how to use scenario modeling to plan smarter financial moves, and how to ensure you never again face a shocking tax bill. This is the bridge between earning money and keeping it. Artificial intelligence now gives you the power to see the future of your taxes—and to change it before it arrives.

Chapter 1

The End of Tax Surprises: How AI Predicts Your Tax Future

For most of modern history, personal taxes have operated like a financial ambush. You work all year, earn income, pay bills, maybe save a little, and then months later you are told whether you made the right moves or not. The problem is not that taxes are complicated—it is that the feedback loop is broken. Humans only get results long after decisions are made. Artificial intelligence changes this by restoring instant feedback to the tax system. Instead of discovering the consequences of your income and spending after the year is over, AI models can now forecast those consequences in real time, turning tax planning into a living, ongoing process rather than a once-a-year event.

At the core of AI tax forecasting is predictive modeling. These systems do not just record what happened; they learn from patterns across millions of taxpayers, historical IRS rules, income behaviors, and economic data. When your income changes, your AI system immediately understands how that change ripples through your tax brackets, credits, phaseouts, and deductions. It projects what your tax liability will look like at the end of the year if you continue on the same path, allowing you to adjust long before damage occurs. This is similar to how modern navigation apps reroute drivers in real time to avoid traffic, except here the traffic jam is an unexpected tax bill.

One of the most powerful aspects of AI forecasting is its ability to unify all income streams into one coherent picture. In the modern economy, most people no longer have just one paycheck. They have wages, freelance income, investment income, crypto gains, rental profits, and sometimes even international earnings. Each stream is taxed differently, and each affects your marginal tax rate. Traditional tools struggle to connect all of this, but AI sees it as a single system. It calculates how one additional dollar earned from any source changes your entire tax profile, allowing you to optimize how and when income is received.

AI also understands time in a way humans and spreadsheets do not. It knows that earning an extra $10,000 in January versus December can produce very different tax outcomes when it comes to withholding, estimated payments, penalties, and cash flow. By forecasting forward week by week and month by month, AI can recommend not only how much you should earn but when you should earn it. This transforms tax planning into a scheduling strategy, where income timing becomes just as important as income itself. Another critical advantage is AI's ability to simulate thousands of alternative futures. You can ask, "What happens if I take a new contract?" "What if I sell a rental?" "What if I increase my retirement contributions?" The AI instantly calculates how each choice changes your tax liability. This allows you to choose the version of the future that keeps the most money in your pocket. Instead of hoping you made the right choice, you know before you act.

This predictive power makes withholding optimization possible. Most people have taxes withheld based on outdated assumptions from when they started a job. AI continuously recalculates what should be withheld based on your current income mix. If you start earning freelance income, the AI detects under-withholding and recommends increasing paycheck withholding or estimated payments. If your income drops, it prevents over-withholding so you keep more of your money. This creates a balance where you neither owe nor overpay.

AI also adapts to tax law changes automatically. When the IRS updates brackets, credits, or deductions, AI models update their forecasts instantly. This means your tax plan never becomes outdated. Instead of scrambling to understand new rules, you benefit from them the moment they take effect. This gives ordinary taxpayers the same kind of real-time tax intelligence once reserved for high-net-worth individuals and corporate finance departments. What makes this truly revolutionary is how accessible it has become. AI tax forecasting is no longer reserved for accountants with expensive software. It is now built into modern tax platforms, financial apps, and personal finance dashboards. Everyday workers, freelancers, and investors can see their tax future as clearly as their bank balance. This democratization of forecasting shifts power away from institutions and back to individuals.

By the end of this book, you will understand how these systems work, how to connect them to your income sources, and how to use them to eliminate surprises, penalties, and wasted refunds. You will no longer be guessing what April will bring. You will already know—and you will be in control of it.

"The Year Elena Finally Kept Her Money"

Elena had always feared tax season. Every spring, it felt like a judgment day where she discovered whether she had lived her financial life correctly or not. Sometimes she owed thousands, sometimes she got a refund, but it was always a surprise. When she started freelancing on top of her regular job, the anxiety became worse. She never knew how much of her income actually belonged to her. Then one day, a friend showed her an AI tax forecasting app that changed everything.

At first, Elena was skeptical. She connected her paycheck, her freelance payments, and her investment accounts, expecting another useless estimate. But the dashboard showed something different. It showed her projected tax bill for December, updated every day. She could see how a freelance project would increase her tax, and how a retirement contribution would reduce it. It was like seeing into the future.

A month later, Elena landed a big contract. Normally she would have celebrated and spent the money. Instead, she checked her AI forecast. It showed that without adjusting withholding, she would owe over $6,000 at tax time. The system recommended increasing her paycheck withholding and setting aside a specific amount from each freelance payment. She followed the guidance, and for the first time in her life, she felt calm about earning more money.

As the year went on, Elena started experimenting with scenarios. She tested what would happen if she took a vacation, bought new equipment, or invested in stocks. Each time, the AI showed her the tax impact instantly. She began making smarter decisions, not because she knew tax law, but because she could see the consequences in advance.

In the fall, Elena's income dipped slightly. In the past, she would have kept overpaying taxes without realizing it. But her

AI detected the change and recommended reducing her withholding so she could keep more of her paycheck. The money helped her through a tight month without touching her savings.

By December, Elena opened her forecast and smiled. It showed that she would owe almost nothing and get almost nothing back. For the first time, she had used her money all year instead of lending it to the government. When she filed her return in April, there were no shocks, no panic, and no stress—just confirmation of what she already knew.

Elena realized that she had not become a tax expert. She had simply gained a window into the future. And with that window, she had finally taken control of her financial life.

Chapter 2

Real-Time Income Mapping: How AI Tracks Every Dollar Before the IRS Does

The foundation of accurate tax forecasting is not guessing or estimation—it is visibility. The IRS sees your income through delayed forms, quarterly reports, and year-end filings, but artificial intelligence sees it the moment it is earned. Real-time income mapping allows AI systems to connect directly to payroll platforms, gig economy apps, investment accounts, crypto wallets, and business payment processors so that every dollar is categorized and analyzed instantly. This creates a continuously updated financial picture that becomes the backbone of accurate tax prediction and withholding optimization.

Traditional tax planning operates on static snapshots. You earn money, record it later, and only see how it affects your taxes long after the opportunity to adjust has passed. AI replaces this with a live model of your financial life. When a paycheck arrives, the system updates your projected annual income. When a freelance invoice is paid, it adjusts your marginal tax rate. When a dividend posts or a crypto trade settles, the forecast changes again. This living model allows you to see how today's income will shape your tax situation months into the future.

AI does not merely record income—it understands its tax character. Wages, self-employment income, rental profits, capital gains, dividends, and interest are all taxed differently. AI categorizes each dollar based on its source, applies the correct tax treatment, and integrates it into your overall tax model. This prevents one of the most common problems in tax planning: treating all income as if it were the same when it is not. The result is dramatically more accurate forecasting and smarter withholding recommendations.

One of the biggest challenges for people with multiple income streams is uneven cash flow. A freelancer might earn nothing one month and a large sum the next. A real estate investor might receive rent steadily but sell a property once a year. AI tracks these fluctuations and smooths them into a coherent annual forecast. It can recommend how much to set aside from each payment so that taxes remain balanced throughout the year instead of becoming a crushing burden all at once.

This real-time mapping also protects you from silent tax creep. When income rises slowly, many people do not realize they have crossed into a higher tax bracket or lost eligibility for certain credits. AI catches this immediately. It alerts you when your income is approaching a threshold that will increase your taxes, giving you the opportunity to adjust withholding, increase deductions, or shift income timing to avoid unnecessary tax increases.

AI systems also integrate employer withholding data. They compare what is being taken out of your paycheck with what should be taken out based on your actual income and tax profile. If the numbers drift apart, the AI flags the difference and recommends corrections. This closes the gap between reality and withholding, preventing the slow accumulation of underpayment or overpayment that leads to tax surprises.

Another powerful feature is cross-account reconciliation. AI checks your bank deposits, payment processors, and reported income to ensure that nothing is missing. This is especially important for freelancers and business owners, where unreported income can trigger audits and penalties. By catching discrepancies early, AI keeps your tax forecast aligned with what the IRS will eventually see.

Real-time income mapping also enables cash-flow-based tax planning. Instead of guessing how much you can afford to set aside for taxes, AI calculates it precisely. It knows your income patterns, expenses, and tax obligations, allowing it to recommend the exact amount you should reserve from each payment. This ensures you always have the money available when taxes are due without starving your day-to-day finances. As you move through this book, you will learn how to connect your income sources to AI tax systems, how to interpret their dashboards, and how to use real-time income data to make smarter financial decisions. When every dollar is mapped, nothing is left to chance—and tax control becomes automatic.

"The Dashboard That Never Slept"

Marcus had always lived with financial uncertainty. His income came from everywhere—ride-share driving, freelance design, rental property, and occasional stock trades. Some months he felt rich, and other months he struggled. But the worst part was never knowing how much he truly earned after taxes. Then he signed up for an AI tax forecasting platform that promised to track every dollar in real time.

At first, Marcus simply watched the dashboard out of curiosity. Every time a ride-share payment hit his account, the number on his screen changed. When a tenant paid rent, his annual income projection jumped. When he sold a stock, the system immediately showed how much of the gain belonged to him and how much belonged to the IRS. For the first time, his chaotic income made sense.

One day, Marcus noticed an alert. His income had quietly pushed him into a higher tax bracket. Without the AI, he would never have known until tax season. The system recommended increasing his estimated payments and adjusting his paycheck withholding from a small part-time job. He followed the instructions, and the future tax spike disappeared.

Later that year, Marcus landed a big freelance contract. The AI showed him exactly how much to set aside from each payment so he would not be hit with a massive bill later. Instead of guessing, he followed the numbers. The money went into a separate savings account, calmly accumulating.

When his rental property needed repairs, Marcus worried about cash flow. The AI recalculated his tax reserves and showed him he could safely use part of the tax savings without risking penalties. The system adapted instantly, giving him flexibility without fear.

By the end of the year, Marcus realized something had changed. He no longer feared income spikes or surprise expenses. Every dollar was mapped. Every future tax bill was visible. When April arrived, his return matched the forecast almost perfectly.

The dashboard had done more than track his money—it had given him peace.

Chapter 3

Dynamic Withholding: How AI Adjusts Your Taxes Before Problems Appear

Withholding was designed for a world where people had one job, one paycheck, and one predictable income stream. In that world, filling out a W-4 once every few years made sense. But modern income is fluid. People change jobs, earn bonuses, take on side gigs, invest in crypto, collect rent, and receive unpredictable payments. Static withholding cannot keep up with this reality. Artificial intelligence solves this by turning withholding into a dynamic, continuously optimized system that adjusts automatically as your financial life changes.

Dynamic withholding begins with real-time income forecasting. Once AI knows how much you are likely to earn for the year, it calculates exactly how much tax should be paid across all income sources. It then compares that number to what is currently being withheld from your paycheck and paid through estimated payments. If the system detects a gap, it generates recommendations to close it—either by increasing or decreasing withholding or adjusting how much you set aside from variable income. This ensures that your tax position remains balanced throughout the year. One of the biggest advantages of AI-driven withholding is that it prevents underpayment penalties before they ever arise. The IRS requires that you pay in a certain percentage of your tax liability throughout the year. When income spikes unexpectedly, many people unknowingly fall below these thresholds. AI systems track these requirements automatically and alert you the moment you are at risk. This allows you to correct course with a simple adjustment instead of facing penalties months later.

AI also eliminates over-withholding, one of the most common and expensive mistakes taxpayers make. When too much tax is taken out, you lose the ability to use that money for investing, debt reduction, or living expenses. AI continuously checks whether you are on track for a large refund and, if so, recommends reducing withholding so you keep more of your money now instead of waiting for it later. This improves cash flow without increasing risk.

Another key benefit of dynamic withholding is that it adapts to life changes instantly. Marriage, divorce, having children, changing jobs, starting a business, or retiring all dramatically change your tax situation. AI detects these changes through income patterns and account connections and updates your withholding strategy accordingly. You no longer have to remember to update forms or guess how a life event will affect your taxes—the system handles it for you. Dynamic withholding also works across multiple income streams. If you have a W-2 job, freelance income, and investment income, AI coordinates all of them into one unified strategy. It might recommend higher withholding on your paycheck to cover taxes from freelance work or suggest quarterly payments for investment income. The goal is to distribute your tax payments in the least disruptive way possible while keeping you compliant.

This system creates a new level of financial stability. Instead of fearing big bills or hoping for refunds, you operate in a narrow, predictable range. You always know where you stand, and small adjustments keep everything on track. Taxes become another manageable monthly expense instead of a once-a-year crisis.

By mastering dynamic withholding, you gain the ability to control your tax cash flow with precision. AI does not remove taxes, but it removes the chaos. It ensures that every dollar you owe is planned for—and every dollar you do not owe stays in your pocket.

"The Adjustment That Saved Jordan"

Jordan thought he had his finances under control. He had a steady job, a side consulting business, and a small investment portfolio. But one year, his consulting income doubled. He was thrilled—until tax season arrived and he was hit with a massive bill and penalties for underpayment. The experience left him frustrated and wary of earning more money.

The following year, Jordan tried something new. He connected his accounts to an AI tax system that offered dynamic withholding. At first, it simply observed his income. Then, as his consulting payments increased, the system sent a notification. It showed him that he was on track to underpay and recommended a small increase in his paycheck withholding to compensate.

Jordan followed the instructions, and nothing dramatic happened. He barely noticed the change. But every time his consulting income fluctuated, the AI quietly adjusted the numbers behind the scenes. When business slowed, it reduced withholding. When a big contract came in, it raised it again.

Midway through the year, Jordan checked his dashboard. It showed he was perfectly on track—no penalties, no big refund, no looming bill. For the first time, his income growth was not creating financial anxiety.

When April arrived, Jordan filed his return and owed almost nothing. There were no penalties, no scrambling, and no stress. He realized that the AI had not changed how much tax he paid—it had changed when and how he paid it.

And that made all the difference.

Chapter 4

Scenario Modeling: How AI Lets You Test the Future Before You Live It

One of the greatest weaknesses in traditional tax planning is that it assumes the future will look exactly like the past. Most tax advice is based on what already happened, not what might happen next. This forces people to make financial decisions in the dark, hoping the outcome will be manageable when tax season arrives. Artificial intelligence eliminates this blind spot through scenario modeling—the ability to simulate multiple possible futures and see their tax consequences before a single decision is finalized. Instead of reacting to outcomes, you are now choosing between them.

Scenario modeling works by creating parallel versions of your financial life. The AI takes your current income, expenses, assets, deductions, credits, and withholding data, then projects forward under different assumptions. What if your income increases by ten percent? What if you take on a new client? What if you sell an investment, buy property, contribute more to retirement, or change jobs? Each scenario is processed instantly, with the AI recalculating your tax liability, withholding needs, and cash flow impact for the rest of the year. This allows you to see not just whether a decision is profitable, but whether it is tax-efficient.

This capability is especially powerful because taxes are nonlinear. A small change in income can trigger outsized effects—higher marginal tax rates, loss of credits, Medicare surcharges, or additional taxes on investment income. Humans are notoriously bad at predicting these thresholds, but AI excels at them. Scenario modeling reveals hidden cliffs and phaseouts before you step over them. Instead of accidentally crossing a line that costs you thousands, you can restructure income timing, deductions, or withholding to soften or eliminate the impact.

AI scenario modeling also introduces timing as a strategic tool. Many financial decisions are not just about what you do, but when you do it. Selling an asset in December versus January, taking a bonus this year versus next, or accelerating deductions before year-end can dramatically change your tax outcome. AI allows you to test these timing decisions side by side. You can see which version of the future leaves you with more cash, less stress, and better long-term positioning.

Another critical advantage is emotional clarity. Financial decisions are often driven by fear or excitement rather than logic. Scenario modeling grounds those emotions in numbers. When you can see that a decision increases your tax bill by a manageable amount—or avoids a major penalty—you gain confidence. When you see that a seemingly attractive move creates long-term tax drag, you can pause and rethink. This replaces guesswork with informed choice.

Scenario modeling is also cumulative. You are not limited to testing one decision at a time. AI can simulate layered futures: new income plus new investments plus retirement contributions plus changes in withholding. This holistic approach mirrors real life, where decisions rarely occur in isolation. The result is a strategic overview of your entire financial trajectory, not just isolated tax estimates.

Perhaps most importantly, scenario modeling shifts taxes from a constraint into a design element. Instead of asking, “Can I afford this after taxes?” you begin asking, “How do I structure this to minimize taxes?” AI gives you the tools to answer that question with precision. You are no longer at the mercy of the tax code—you are navigating it intentionally.

By mastering AI-driven scenario modeling, you gain the ability to explore the future safely. You can test decisions without consequences, learn without penalties, and choose the path that aligns best with your goals. Taxes stop being a surprise and become a variable you control.

"Seven Futures, One Choice"

When Daniel first heard about AI scenario modeling, he dismissed it as another financial buzzword. He was forty-three, had a stable job in logistics, a growing side business, and a modest investment portfolio. On paper, he was doing well. But every major financial decision he made seemed to come with an invisible tax consequence that only revealed itself months later. He had learned to live with uncertainty, but he never liked it.

Everything changed the year his company offered him a promotion that included a substantial bonus and stock compensation. The offer was exciting, but it came with complexity. He would earn more, but he did not know how much more he would actually keep. At the same time, his side business was growing, and he was considering selling a rental property he had owned for years. Too many decisions. Too many unknowns.

Out of curiosity, Daniel signed up for an AI tax forecasting platform that included scenario modeling. He connected his accounts and waited as the system built a digital version of his financial life. When the dashboard appeared, it showed his projected tax outcome if he did nothing. It was fine—but it was only one future. The AI prompted him to explore alternatives. Daniel created his first scenario: accepting the promotion as offered. Instantly, the numbers changed. His income rose sharply, but so did his taxes. The AI highlighted a hidden issue—his bonus would push him into a higher marginal bracket and trigger additional taxes on his investment income. The increase was not catastrophic, but it was larger than he expected.

In the second scenario, Daniel adjusted the timing of the bonus, splitting it across two years. The AI recalculated again. This time, the tax spike softened. He stayed below certain thresholds, saving thousands. Daniel felt a small thrill. For the first time, he was not guessing—he was seeing.

Then he tested a third future: accepting the promotion and selling the rental property in the same year. The AI lit up with warnings. Capital gains taxes stacked on top of higher income created a massive tax burden. In this future, Daniel owed far more than he was comfortable with. He leaned back in his chair, realizing how close he had come to making a costly mistake.

In the fourth scenario, he delayed the property sale by one year. The difference was dramatic. The AI showed him that spacing out the income allowed him to manage withholding smoothly and avoid penalties. The future looked calmer, cleaner, and more predictable.

Curious now, Daniel kept going. In the fifth scenario, he added increased retirement contributions. The AI showed how this not only reduced his taxable income but also brought his withholding back into balance. The system recommended precise adjustments to his paycheck withholding to align everything perfectly.

In the sixth scenario, Daniel imagined turning his side business into a full-time operation. The AI simulated estimated payments, self-employment taxes, and cash flow needs. The numbers were intimidating—but clear. For the first time, the risk felt measurable instead of frightening.

Finally, Daniel created a seventh scenario: a carefully designed path combining the promotion, delayed property sale, optimized retirement contributions, and dynamic withholding adjustments. The AI recalculated one last time. This future showed stability, controlled taxes, no penalties, and strong cash flow throughout the year.

Daniel stared at the screen for a long time. Seven futures had unfolded in front of him, each with different consequences. Only one felt right.

Months later, Daniel followed the plan he had chosen. When life unfolded as predicted, there was no shock. His withholding adjusted smoothly. His cash flow remained steady. When tax season arrived, the numbers matched the forecast almost exactly. Daniel realized something profound. The AI had not told him what to do. It had simply shown him the future—and let him choose wisely.

Chapter 5

Penalty Prevention & Cash Flow Control: How AI Keeps You Compliant Without Stress

For most taxpayers, penalties are not the result of wrongdoing. They are the result of misalignment—earning income faster than taxes are being paid, misunderstanding payment thresholds, or assuming everything will balance out at the end of the year. The IRS penalty system is largely invisible until it is triggered, and by the time it appears, it is already too late to undo. Artificial intelligence fundamentally changes this dynamic by monitoring compliance continuously, identifying risk early, and guiding corrective action long before penalties become unavoidable.

At the heart of penalty prevention is understanding that the IRS expects taxes to be paid as income is earned, not all at once. This expectation applies whether income comes from wages, self-employment, investments, or a combination of sources. AI systems are built to track this requirement automatically. They compare your projected annual tax liability against what has already been paid through withholding and estimated payments. When the system detects that payments are falling behind required thresholds, it flags the issue immediately and offers specific, actionable recommendations to fix it.

One of the most valuable aspects of AI-driven penalty prevention is its ability to translate complex IRS rules into simple guidance. Safe harbor thresholds, quarterly payment requirements, and underpayment calculations are notoriously confusing. AI abstracts this complexity away from the user. Instead of forcing you to understand the rules, it simply tells you what action is needed and when. This removes fear and replaces it with clarity.

AI also excels at managing uneven income. Many penalties occur because income arrives in bursts—bonuses, commissions, contract payments, asset sales—without corresponding tax payments. AI systems smooth these spikes across the year, calculating how much should be set aside or paid immediately to stay compliant. This prevents the common trap of spending income first and worrying about taxes later.

Cash flow control is the second major benefit of AI-driven tax optimization. Paying taxes early or overpaying can be just as damaging as underpaying. When too much money is locked up with the government, it cannot be used for investing, debt reduction, or living expenses. AI monitors this balance constantly. If it detects that you are on track for a large refund, it recommends reducing withholding so you can reclaim control of your cash without increasing risk.

What makes AI particularly powerful is its ability to coordinate penalty prevention with lifestyle reality. It understands not just tax rules, but timing, liquidity, and financial strain. If income drops temporarily, AI recalculates payment schedules to avoid unnecessary stress while still maintaining compliance. This creates a tax strategy that is flexible, humane, and responsive to real life.

AI also provides psychological relief. Penalties create anxiety because they are unpredictable and poorly understood. When AI handles compliance in the background, tax fear fades. You are no longer wondering whether you have paid enough or whether a bill is coming. You know—because the system is watching continuously.

This chapter teaches you how AI identifies penalty risk, how it calculates required payments, and how it integrates tax obligations into everyday cash flow planning. When penalties are prevented automatically and cash flow is optimized intelligently, taxes stop being a source of fear and become just another managed variable in your financial life.

"The Letter That Never Came"

For years, Vanessa believed tax penalties were inevitable. She had never intentionally avoided paying taxes, yet every few years a letter arrived that made her stomach drop. It always said the same thing in slightly different language: underpayment, interest, penalty due. The amounts varied, but the feeling never did. A quiet shame mixed with frustration. She paid the bill, promised herself she would do better next year, and then watched the cycle repeat.

Vanessa's income was the problem—at least that was what she told herself. She worked in marketing, earned a salary, but also took on consulting projects when opportunities appeared. Some months she earned much more than others. The extra income felt like a reward for working harder, yet it always seemed to come with a hidden cost she could not quite predict or control.

The worst year came after a particularly successful stretch. She had landed two large consulting clients while still working full time. She felt proud, accomplished, and optimistic—until tax season arrived. The bill was larger than ever, and this time it included penalties and interest. She paid it, but the emotional toll lingered. She began associating growth with punishment.

The following spring, a colleague mentioned using an AI tax system that handled forecasting and compliance automatically. Vanessa listened politely but remained skeptical. She had tried spreadsheets, budgeting apps, even professional help. Nothing had prevented the penalties. Still, the phrase “penalty prevention” stayed with her.

She signed up quietly, without much expectation. The setup process was simple. She connected her payroll, consulting income, bank accounts, and prior tax history. When the dashboard appeared, it showed something unfamiliar: a compliance meter. Green, yellow, red. At the moment, she was green.

Weeks passed. Vanessa forgot about the system until one afternoon a notification appeared. It was calm, almost gentle. It explained that her recent consulting payment had pushed her projected tax payments below the IRS safe threshold. It did not panic. It did not threaten. It simply recommended a small estimated payment and a temporary increase in withholding.

Vanessa hesitated. In the past, this was the point where she would ignore the issue and hope for the best. This time, she followed the instructions. The payment was manageable. The withholding change barely affected her paycheck.

As the months passed, the system continued to watch quietly. When income increased, it adjusted. When income slowed, it eased off. Vanessa noticed something subtle but powerful: she was never surprised. There were no shocks, no sudden realizations that she had fallen behind. Everything unfolded gradually, predictably.

Midyear, an unexpected expense hit—a family emergency that required travel and time off. Vanessa worried about cash flow. She opened the AI dashboard, expecting bad news. Instead, it recalculated her tax position and showed her exactly how much flexibility she had. It even recommended temporarily reducing withholding to ease the strain without creating compliance risk. She followed the guidance and felt immediate relief.

By autumn, Vanessa realized she had stopped worrying about taxes entirely. The fear that once lived quietly in the back of her mind was gone. Income felt like income again—not a prelude to punishment.

When December arrived, Vanessa checked her dashboard one last time. It showed a narrow range: she would owe a small amount or receive a small refund. Either way, there would be no penalties. No interest. No letters.

April came and went quietly. Vanessa filed her return and waited. Nothing happened. No envelope. No warning. No sinking feeling.

Weeks later, she realized the significance of what had not occurred. The letter had never come.

For the first time in her adult life, Vanessa understood that penalties were not inevitable. They were preventable. And with the right system watching the future on her behalf, growth no longer felt dangerous. It felt free.

Chapter 6

Year-Round Tax Orchestration: How AI Turns Taxes Into a Monthly Strategy

Most people experience taxes as an annual interruption to their lives rather than an integrated part of their financial system. They earn, spend, save, and invest for twelve months, then abruptly stop to reconstruct what happened for the IRS. This separation is the root cause of tax stress. Artificial intelligence eliminates this divide by transforming taxes into a year-round orchestration—an ongoing, adaptive strategy that evolves monthly, weekly, and sometimes daily as financial activity occurs. Instead of preparing for taxes, you are continuously managing them.

Year-round tax orchestration begins by treating taxes as a living system rather than a static obligation. AI models do not wait for forms or deadlines. They observe patterns, trends, and momentum in income and expenses, updating forecasts continuously. Every paycheck, transaction, contribution, and investment decision feeds into the model, allowing it to maintain a constantly refreshed projection of tax liability. This shifts tax planning from hindsight to foresight. One of the most important elements of orchestration is rhythm. Taxes are not meant to be paid in a single dramatic moment. They are meant to flow gradually alongside income. AI establishes this rhythm by coordinating withholding, estimated payments, deductions, and credits into a steady cadence. When income rises, payments adjust. When income slows, the system eases pressure. This prevents the emotional whiplash of sudden bills or unexpected refunds.

AI also integrates taxes with broader financial planning. Retirement contributions, health savings accounts, education expenses, charitable giving, and investment strategies all have tax consequences. In a year-round system, these are not separate decisions. AI evaluates them together, showing how each move affects the whole. This allows individuals to optimize not just taxes, but overall financial efficiency.

Another key feature of year-round orchestration is adaptability. Life does not follow neat financial plans. Jobs change, businesses grow or shrink, emergencies arise, and opportunities appear unexpectedly. AI responds to these changes instantly. It recalculates projections, updates compliance status, and recommends adjustments without requiring the user to stop and rethink everything. Taxes stay aligned even when life does not.

This orchestration also reduces cognitive burden. Most people do not want to think about taxes every month. AI allows them not to. Once the system is in place, it operates quietly in the background, surfacing information only when action is needed. Instead of constant vigilance, users experience calm awareness—knowing that nothing is being missed.

Perhaps the most transformative effect of year-round orchestration is confidence. When taxes are managed continuously, fear disappears. There is no dread of unknown outcomes, no anxiety about mistakes, and no rush to fix problems at the last minute. Taxes become predictable, manageable, and integrated into everyday life.

By the end of this chapter, you will understand how AI coordinates taxes across the entire year, how monthly adjustments prevent annual chaos, and how to move from reactive filing to proactive orchestration. This is where tax optimization becomes sustainable—not just for one year, but for a lifetime.

"A Year Without April"

Sophia used to measure her year in deadlines. Work deadlines. Family deadlines. And looming over all of them, the invisible deadline of tax season. April was never just a month—it was a mood. Anxiety crept in quietly after the holidays and grew louder as spring approached. Even when she filed on time, she never felt prepared. Taxes always seemed to arrive like an exam she had not studied for.

Sophia's financial life was not unusual, but it was layered. She worked in product management, received bonuses, invested regularly, and earned occasional income consulting for startups. Some years were smooth. Others were chaotic. The only constant was uncertainty. She never knew how much she truly had until the tax return told her.

One winter, after a particularly exhausting tax season, Sophia decided she was done with the cycle. She did not want to become a tax expert. She wanted a system—something that would quietly handle the complexity without demanding her constant attention. That was when she discovered AI-driven year-round tax orchestration.

At first, the idea felt abstract. Taxes had always been something she dealt with once a year. The concept of managing them continuously seemed excessive. Still, she signed up. She connected her income sources, investments, and prior returns. The system took time to learn her patterns. Sophia watched with mild curiosity, not yet convinced.

January passed. February arrived. Nothing dramatic happened. The dashboard showed projections, but Sophia did not obsess over them. March came—and for the first time in her adult life, she did not feel the familiar tightening in her chest. There was no rush. No panic. She already knew what her tax outcome would be.

As the year unfolded, the system worked quietly. When Sophia received a bonus, it adjusted her withholding. When her consulting income dipped, it recalculated her estimated payments. When she increased her retirement contributions, the forecast updated instantly. Taxes were no longer something that waited in the future—they moved alongside her life, step by step.

Midyear, Sophia faced an unexpected decision. A startup she had advised offered her equity in exchange for continued consulting. In the past, she would have hesitated, worried about the tax implications. This time, she ran a scenario. The AI showed her how the equity would affect her taxes now and later. It recommended specific adjustments to keep everything balanced. The decision felt informed instead of risky.

Summer passed. Fall arrived. Sophia realized something strange: she had stopped thinking about taxes entirely. Not because she was ignoring them—but because they were already accounted for. The system surfaced only what mattered, when it mattered. The rest faded into the background.

In December, Sophia reviewed the year. Her income had grown. Her investments had performed well. Her cash flow had remained steady. Taxes had not once disrupted her plans. There had been no scrambling, no surprises, no guilt, no fear.

April came quietly. Sophia filed her return almost absentmindedly. The numbers matched what she already knew. No shock. No stress. No emotional spike. Just confirmation.

Weeks later, Sophia realized she had not noticed April at all. It had passed like any other month.

For the first time, her year had not revolved around tax season. It had simply flowed.

Sophia smiled at the thought. She had not eliminated taxes. She had eliminated the drama.

And once that was gone, the rest of her life felt lighter.

Chapter 7

From Guesswork to Precision: Building a Personal AI Tax Command Center

The final transformation in AI tax forecasting is not technological—it is psychological. The moment a person stops guessing about taxes and starts seeing them clearly, everything changes. Taxes cease to be a background threat and become an engineered system. This shift happens when individuals move from passive awareness to active oversight by building what can best be described as a personal AI tax command center: a centralized environment where income, withholding, forecasting, compliance, and decision-making converge into a single, continuously updated source of truth.

A tax command center is not about obsessing over numbers. It is about consolidating fragmented financial information into a coherent, interpretable model. Historically, tax data has lived in silos—pay stubs in one place, bank accounts in another, investment statements somewhere else, and tax returns stored away once a year. AI collapses these silos. It ingests data from every relevant source, normalizes it, and translates it into a unified projection of tax reality. This removes the fog that causes mistakes and anxiety. Precision is the defining advantage of this approach. Instead of vague estimates, AI systems calculate exact ranges, probabilities, and thresholds. They show not only what is likely to happen, but why. When a forecast changes, the system explains which variables caused the shift—income increases, deduction changes, law updates, or timing adjustments. This transparency builds trust and understanding, allowing users to act with confidence rather than fear.

A personal tax command center also introduces intentional control. With AI continuously monitoring the system, users can choose when to intervene and when to let automation handle the details. Adjustments to withholding, estimated payments, or savings strategies are no longer reactive emergencies. They are small, deliberate corrections applied early and gently. This keeps the system stable and predictable over time.

Another critical element is learning. Over time, the AI observes how the user responds to recommendations, which strategies are preferred, and how risk tolerance manifests. The system adapts accordingly. For conservative users, it may prioritize safety margins. For aggressive earners, it may focus on maximizing liquidity while staying compliant. The result is a tax strategy that feels personal, not generic.

The command center also acts as a buffer between the user

and complexity. Tax laws, thresholds, and rules change constantly. Instead of forcing individuals to keep up, AI absorbs the complexity and updates the model automatically. The user sees outcomes, not statutes. This makes precision sustainable year after year, even as rules evolve.

Ultimately, building a personal AI tax command center is about reclaiming agency. It restores the connection between effort and reward. When people can see how much they earn, how much they owe, and how to optimize the difference, money becomes less abstract and more purposeful. Taxes no longer distort decision-making—they inform it.

This chapter represents the culmination of AI tax forecasting and withholding optimization. It is where all previous concepts—real-time mapping, dynamic withholding, scenario modeling, penalty prevention, and year-round orchestration—converge into a single, integrated system. With a command center in place, tax outcomes are no longer surprises. They are designed.

"The Screen That Changed Everything"

Ethan had always considered himself responsible with money, but not confident. He paid bills on time, avoided debt, and saved consistently. Still, there was a persistent unease beneath the surface of his financial life—an uncertainty that came from not fully understanding how everything fit together. Taxes were the largest unknown. He knew what he earned, but not what it truly meant.

Every year, Ethan repeated the same ritual. He gathered documents, uploaded forms, answered questions, and waited. Sometimes the result was favorable. Other times it was painful. The outcome felt arbitrary, like rolling dice he did not understand. He told himself this was normal. Everyone dealt with taxes this way.

That belief cracked the year his income changed dramatically. Ethan left a stable corporate role to join a fast-growing company with variable compensation, equity incentives, and performance bonuses. The opportunity excited him, but the uncertainty gnawed at him. He had no idea how much to save, how much to spend, or how much risk he was carrying.

One evening, overwhelmed and restless, Ethan opened his laptop and searched for solutions. That was when he found an AI-driven tax forecasting platform described not as software, but as a "personal tax command center." The phrase intrigued him. He signed up that night.

The setup process was thorough but calm. The system asked for connections—not just income, but accounts, investments, prior returns, and preferences. Ethan felt exposed at first, like he was handing over control. But as the data flowed in, something unexpected happened. The chaos began to organize itself.

When the dashboard appeared, Ethan froze. For the first time, he saw his financial life represented as a system instead of fragments. Income streams converged into a single projection. Withholding appeared as a moving dial. Compliance status displayed quietly in green. The numbers were not scary—they were clear.

Ethan spent hours exploring. He adjusted hypothetical income levels. He tested what would happen if he exercised stock options early or late. He watched the AI explain each outcome in plain language. Every question he had avoided for years finally had an answer.

Over the following months, the command center became a quiet presence in Ethan's life. It did not demand attention. It waited. When income spiked, it suggested adjustments. When decisions loomed, it offered scenarios. Ethan no longer guessed. He chose.

Midyear, Ethan faced a major crossroads. His company offered him an accelerated equity vesting option. In the past, he would have deferred to vague advice and hope. This time, he opened the command center. The AI modeled multiple paths, showing short-term taxes, long-term implications, and cash flow effects. Ethan chose the option that aligned with both his financial goals and his peace of mind.

As the year progressed, something deeper shifted. Ethan noticed he felt calmer. Money decisions no longer carried an emotional charge. He was not avoiding his finances or obsessing over them. He was simply informed.

December arrived, and with it, reflection. Ethan reviewed the year inside the command center. His income had grown. His taxes were fully accounted for. There were no surprises waiting in the future. Everything was already visible.

April came and went quietly. Filing felt procedural, almost boring. The results matched the forecast within a narrow margin. No shock. No regret. No relief—because there had been no fear.

One evening, months later, Ethan sat at his desk and stared at the screen that had changed everything. It was not flashy. It did not promise miracles. It simply showed the truth.

And for the first time, that was enough.

Ethan closed his laptop, confident not just in his numbers—but in himself.

Chapter 8

Staying Ahead of Change: How AI Adapts to Tax Law, Income Shifts, and Life Events

One of the most dangerous assumptions taxpayers make is believing that once a tax plan is set, it will remain valid. In reality, tax outcomes are fragile. They are shaped not only by income, but by constantly shifting variables—tax law updates, economic changes, employer policy adjustments, market fluctuations, and life events that arrive without warning. Traditional tax planning fails because it treats change as an exception. Artificial intelligence succeeds because it treats change as the norm. AI-driven tax forecasting systems are built to absorb disruption, recalibrate instantly, and maintain alignment even when the ground is moving beneath you.

Tax law itself is a living system. Brackets shift, credits phase in and out, thresholds adjust for inflation, and entire rulesets can change through legislation or regulation. Humans struggle to keep pace with this evolution, especially when changes are subtle or buried in technical language. AI systems monitor these changes continuously, updating their internal models the moment new rules take effect. This ensures that forecasts remain accurate without requiring users to track legislative developments or interpret complex guidance.

Income volatility is another constant source of risk. Even people with stable jobs experience fluctuations through bonuses, commissions, overtime, stock compensation, or side income. Others face far greater variability—freelancers, business owners, investors, and gig workers whose income may rise or fall dramatically within short periods. AI is uniquely equipped to handle this volatility because it recalculates projections dynamically. Instead of assuming stability, it anticipates movement and adjusts withholding, estimated payments, and compliance thresholds accordingly.

Life events introduce even more complexity. Marriage, divorce, childbirth, relocation, career changes, illness, inheritance, and retirement all carry tax consequences that ripple across multiple years. AI systems detect these changes through shifts in financial behavior and account data, then reconfigure forecasts to reflect the new reality. This prevents the common problem of operating under outdated assumptions long after life has changed.

Adaptability also extends to behavioral patterns. AI learns how individuals interact with their finances—how aggressively they save, how quickly they respond to recommendations, and how much risk they are comfortable carrying. Over time, the system refines its guidance to better match the user's preferences. This personalization makes tax optimization sustainable, not burdensome.

Another key strength of AI adaptation is resilience. When unexpected events occur—market downturns, sudden income loss, emergency expenses—AI does not panic. It recalculates. It shows what is still safe, what needs adjustment, and what can be deferred without creating future problems. This prevents knee-jerk decisions driven by fear and replaces them with measured responses grounded in data.

Staying ahead of change is not about predicting every event. It is about building a system that responds intelligently when events occur. AI provides this responsiveness. It ensures that tax strategy remains aligned not just with who you were at the beginning of the year, but with who you are becoming as the year unfolds.

This chapter completes the architecture of AI tax forecasting by addressing the final challenge: uncertainty. With AI continuously adapting to law, income, and life itself, taxes no longer break when plans change. They bend, adjust, and remain under control.

"The Year Everything Changed"

When Maya looked back on her life, she would later divide it into two parts: before that year, and after it. At the time, she had no idea it would become a dividing line. She entered the year expecting routine—steady work, predictable income, and familiar responsibilities. She exited it transformed, not just by what had happened, but by how she had navigated it.

Maya worked as a project manager for a mid-sized healthcare company. Her income was solid but not extravagant. She lived carefully, saved diligently, and avoided financial surprises whenever possible. Taxes, however, remained her blind spot. She filed on time, paid what she owed, and hoped nothing went wrong. It was not elegant, but it worked.

In January, Maya signed up for an AI tax forecasting platform at the suggestion of her brother, who insisted it had changed the way he thought about money. She was skeptical but curious. She connected her accounts, reviewed the dashboard, and set it aside. Everything looked normal. Predictable. Safe.

Then February arrived with the first change. Her company announced a restructuring that included new bonus structures tied to performance. Maya's income projections shifted overnight. The AI system adjusted immediately, updating her forecast and recommending a modest withholding change.

Maya followed the suggestion without much thought. It felt minor.

In March, a second change arrived—this one personal. Maya's mother fell ill unexpectedly, requiring care and financial support. Maya took time off work and began covering medical expenses. Income dipped. Expenses rose. In the past, this would have triggered panic about taxes. This time, the AI recalculated quietly. It reduced withholding temporarily and showed Maya exactly how much flexibility she had. The numbers were tight, but manageable.

April came with tax law updates—small adjustments tied to inflation and healthcare provisions. Maya barely noticed. The AI absorbed the changes automatically. Her forecast shifted slightly, but nothing broke. She did not read the news. She did not study the rules. She simply stayed aligned.

In early summer, Maya received an unexpected offer. A former colleague invited her to consult on a short-term project that paid well but came with 1099 income. Maya hesitated. In the past, she would have declined, afraid of the tax complexity. Instead, she ran a scenario. The AI showed her how the income would affect her taxes and exactly how much to set aside. The numbers were clear. She accepted. The consulting work was intense but rewarding. Income surged. The AI adjusted withholding and flagged a future estimated payment. Maya followed the guidance. Money moved where it needed to go. There was no guesswork.

In August, the ground shifted again. Maya's company announced layoffs. Her role was safe, but uncertainty spread. Maya opened her dashboard and reviewed multiple futures. What if income dropped? What if she needed to change jobs? What if consulting became her primary income? The AI modeled each path calmly, showing risks and options. Fear gave way to preparation.

September brought another life event. Maya moved closer to her mother to provide care. The relocation affected state taxes and deductions. The AI detected the change through address updates and recalculated everything automatically. Maya did not miss a beat.

By November, Maya realized she had lived through one of the most volatile years of her adult life—and yet, she felt strangely steady. Income had changed. Expenses had surged. Laws had shifted. Life had demanded flexibility. And still, there were no tax emergencies. No looming penalties. No unanswered questions. December arrived quietly. Maya reviewed the year inside her dashboard. The system showed her journey in numbers—peaks, dips, adjustments, adaptations. Everything was accounted for.

April came and went without drama. Filing confirmed what Maya already knew. The forecast had been right.

Later, when someone asked Maya how she stayed calm through such a turbulent year, she paused. The answer was not resilience or discipline or expertise.

It was visibility.

She had not controlled events. She had controlled her response to them.

And that, she realized, had made all the difference.

Chapter 9

From Taxes to Wealth Strategy: How AI Connects Forecasting to Long-Term Financial Power

At a certain level of income and awareness, people begin to realize a subtle truth: taxes are not just an expense, they are a force. They influence how wealth is built, how fast it compounds, and how long it lasts. Traditional tax planning treats taxes as something to minimize year by year, but artificial intelligence enables a more powerful approach—integrating tax forecasting directly into long-term financial strategy. This is where AI tax optimization stops being defensive and becomes generative.

Long-term wealth is shaped by timing, structure, and consistency. When taxes are unpredictable, these elements fracture. People delay investments, hesitate to grow income, or hoard cash out of fear of future liabilities. AI removes this friction by providing continuous clarity. When you can see not only what you owe this year, but how today's decisions affect your tax exposure over five, ten, or twenty years, strategy replaces hesitation. AI accomplishes this by extending forecasting beyond the current tax year. It models future income trajectories, investment growth, retirement timelines, and tax law assumptions to show how wealth evolves under different paths. This allows individuals to compare not just tax outcomes, but net worth outcomes. A strategy that saves a few thousand dollars in taxes today may cost hundreds of thousands in lost compounding later. AI makes these trade-offs visible.

One of the most important applications of this approach is aligning tax strategy with investment strategy. Capital gains, dividends, retirement accounts, real estate depreciation, and business income all interact with the tax system differently over time. AI understands these interactions holistically. It can recommend when to defer taxes, when to realize gains, and when to accelerate deductions based on long-term impact rather than short-term relief.

AI also helps redefine success metrics. Instead of focusing on refunds or bills, the focus shifts to after-tax growth. How much of what you earn actually stays with you? How efficiently does it grow? How resilient is it to change? These questions matter more than any single filing season, and AI places them at the center of financial decision-making.

Another crucial benefit is alignment with life stages. Early career decisions, mid-career expansions, and late-career transitions all carry different tax implications. AI adapts forecasting models to these stages, ensuring that tax strategy evolves alongside goals. What makes sense at thirty does not make sense at fifty, and AI reflects this reality dynamically.

By integrating tax forecasting with long-term planning, AI turns compliance into leverage. Taxes no longer erode wealth silently—they are engineered consciously. This chapter shows how to use AI not just to avoid surprises, but to build enduring financial strength. When taxes are aligned with long-term vision, money works harder, lasts longer, and supports a life designed with intention.

"The Long View"

Nathan used to think of taxes as a yearly inconvenience, something to get through so he could move on with his life. He never imagined they would become one of the most important strategic tools he would ever use. That realization came slowly, shaped not by a single event, but by a sequence of moments that forced him to look further ahead than he ever had before.

Nathan was forty-eight when he began to feel the weight of time. Not in a dramatic way, but in quiet calculations. How many years until retirement? How much was enough? Would his savings hold up? He earned well as a senior engineer, invested consistently, and lived comfortably. On paper, everything was fine. Yet something felt fragile. He could not quite explain it, but he sensed that small inefficiencies—ignored year after year—might add up to something dangerous.

Taxes were part of that unease. Every year, the outcome was different. Sometimes he owed, sometimes he received a refund. He accepted it as normal. What he did not see was how those variations shaped his long-term trajectory.

One evening, while reviewing his investments, Nathan noticed something unsettling. His portfolio had grown, but not as much as expected. The returns were decent, yet the after-tax growth lagged. It was not dramatic, but it was persistent. He began to wonder how much of his effort was being quietly siphoned away.

That curiosity led him to an AI-driven financial platform that promised integrated tax forecasting and long-term modeling. Nathan was skeptical. He was not looking for predictions or gimmicks. He wanted clarity. He wanted to understand the future he was already building.

The setup took time. The system analyzed years of income, investments, tax filings, and savings patterns. When the results appeared, Nathan felt an unexpected jolt. The dashboard did not just show numbers—it showed direction. It projected his net worth across decades under different assumptions. The differences were not subtle.

In one projection, Nathan continued as he always had. The outcome was comfortable but tight. In another, small changes were applied—optimized withholding, adjusted investment timing, strategic tax deferral. The gap between the two futures widened dramatically over time. Hundreds of thousands of dollars separated paths that looked nearly identical in the short term.

Nathan spent days exploring scenarios. What if he delayed certain gains? What if he restructured part of his portfolio? What if he adjusted contributions based on tax efficiency rather than habit? Each scenario unfolded clearly, patiently. The AI did not judge. It simply showed consequences.

What struck Nathan most was how little effort the better path required. It was not about earning more or taking greater risks. It was about alignment. The AI connected decisions across time, showing how today's tax efficiency fed tomorrow's security.

Over the following months, Nathan began to implement changes. Withholding adjusted quietly. Investments were rebalanced with tax impact in mind. Retirement contributions aligned with long-term forecasts. Nothing dramatic happened. Life continued normally.

Yet beneath the surface, something fundamental had shifted. Nathan no longer felt like he was reacting to money. He was directing it. The future no longer felt abstract—it was visible, shaped, and evolving in his favor.

Years passed. Nathan revisited the projections occasionally, not out of anxiety, but curiosity. The forecasts adjusted as life unfolded. Income changed. Markets fluctuated. Laws evolved. The strategy held.

When Nathan finally retired, the transition felt natural. There was no fear of running out, no regret about missed opportunities. The numbers confirmed what he already knew. The long view had paid off.

Looking back, Nathan realized the most powerful change had not been financial. It had been psychological. He had stopped thinking of taxes as something to survive and started treating them as something to design around.

And in doing so, he had quietly, steadily built a future that felt not just secure—but intentional.

Chapter 10

Designing a Stress-Free Financial Life: How AI Makes Tax Certainty Permanent

The ultimate promise of artificial intelligence in personal taxation is not efficiency, accuracy, or even savings—it is certainty. For decades, taxes have been one of the last unpredictable forces in an otherwise digitized financial world. Income could be tracked instantly, investments monitored in real time, and spending categorized automatically, yet taxes still operated on delayed feedback and retroactive judgment. Artificial intelligence closes that gap permanently by transforming tax management from an annual reconciliation into a continuous, predictable system. This is where tax optimization becomes not just a strategy, but a lifestyle.

A stress-free financial life is built on the ability to plan without fear of hidden consequences. When taxes are uncertain, every financial decision carries an invisible risk. People hesitate to earn more, invest boldly, or pursue new opportunities because they do not know what those decisions will cost them later. AI removes this hesitation by making tax outcomes visible in advance. When you know the consequences before you act, confidence replaces anxiety. Permanent tax certainty does not mean static outcomes. Life changes. Income changes. Laws change. What remains constant is awareness. AI provides a continuous signal that tells you where you stand, what is coming, and what—if anything—needs adjustment. Instead of reacting to surprises, you respond to information. This keeps financial stress low even when circumstances are complex.

Another defining feature of AI-driven tax certainty is proportionality. Taxes no longer arrive as dramatic events. They scale smoothly with income, spending, and growth. Payments adjust incrementally. Decisions compound gradually. This eliminates the emotional spikes associated with large bills or unexpected refunds. Money flows in a steady rhythm aligned with real life.

AI also shifts the role of the taxpayer. Instead of being a passive participant subject to rules they barely understand, individuals become designers of their own financial systems. They choose how aggressively to optimize, how conservative to remain, and how much flexibility to preserve. AI adapts to those preferences, ensuring the system supports the person—not the other way around.

Over time, this creates trust—not just in the technology, but in oneself. When people see that outcomes match forecasts year after year, confidence grows. Financial decisions feel grounded rather than speculative. Taxes fade into the background, not because they are ignored, but because they are already handled.

This chapter represents the final step in AI tax forecasting and withholding optimization. It is where the tools, strategies, and systems discussed throughout this book converge into something enduring. A future where taxes are predictable. A present where money decisions are calm. A financial life free from tax-driven stress.

"The Quiet Year"

The year Daniel remembered most was not the one where everything went wrong, nor the one where everything went right. It was the quiet one—the year nothing surprised him.

Daniel had spent most of his adult life bracing himself financially. Not in obvious ways, but subtly. He hesitated before accepting new opportunities. He delayed purchases even when he could afford them. He saved aggressively, not out of discipline, but out of caution. Taxes played a central role in this mindset. They were the unknown variable that made certainty impossible.

Every April reinforced the feeling. Sometimes the outcome was manageable. Other times it was painful. Either way, it always felt final, as though judgment had been passed on decisions made months earlier. Daniel accepted this as adulthood. Responsibility, he told himself, came with uncertainty.

The quiet year began without ceremony. Daniel had already implemented AI-driven tax forecasting the year before, but he did not expect anything profound from it. He simply wanted fewer surprises. The system monitored his income, adjusted withholding, and updated forecasts. It worked—but quietly.

January passed. February arrived. Daniel noticed something unusual: he had not thought about taxes once.

In March, Daniel received a larger-than-expected bonus. In the past, this would have triggered anxiety. How much should he save? How much could he spend? This time, he opened his dashboard. The numbers adjusted instantly. The AI showed him exactly what would change—and what would not. Daniel made a small withholding adjustment and moved on with his day.

Spring brought a personal decision. Daniel and his partner considered moving closer to family. The decision had financial implications—housing costs, commuting, potential tax changes. Daniel ran scenarios. The AI showed the tax impact clearly, without drama. The decision became logistical instead of emotional. Summer arrived with unexpected expenses. A home repair. A medical bill. In previous years, Daniel would have worried about cash flow and future taxes simultaneously. This time, the AI recalculated everything in seconds. The system showed him where flexibility existed. He paid what he needed to pay and slept soundly that night.

As the months passed, Daniel began to notice a shift that was difficult to articulate. Money no longer felt heavy. Decisions no longer felt risky. He was not earning dramatically more, nor spending recklessly. He was simply informed.

In the fall, Daniel reviewed his finances out of habit. The forecast looked stable. There was no looming bill, no hidden risk. Taxes were already accounted for. The future felt... ordinary. And for the first time, that felt extraordinary.

December arrived quietly. Daniel reflected on the year. There had been no financial emergencies. No surprises. No moments of panic. Life had unfolded as life does—messy, imperfect, unpredictable—but his finances had remained calm throughout it.

April came again. Daniel filed his return. The result matched the forecast almost exactly. There was no emotional reaction. No relief. No disappointment. Just confirmation.

Weeks later, Daniel realized something profound. The absence of stress had created space. Space to think creatively. Space to plan. Space to enjoy life without constant calculation.

The quiet year had changed him.

Not because it was dramatic—but because it was predictable.

Daniel closed his laptop one evening and smiled. For the first time, he trusted not just the numbers—but the future they represented.

And that trust, he realized, was the greatest return he had ever earned.

Final Thoughts

Designing the End of Tax Anxiety

The journey through this book has not been about learning tax rules, memorizing regulations, or mastering complex calculations. It has been about changing the relationship between individuals and uncertainty. For decades, taxes have represented one of the last remaining areas of financial life governed by delayed feedback and retroactive judgment. People have been expected to make decisions all year long without knowing their consequences, only to be evaluated months later. Artificial intelligence ends that era.

AI tax forecasting and withholding optimization represent a fundamental shift from reaction to design. Instead of discovering outcomes after the fact, individuals now gain the ability to see forward, adjust early, and remain aligned throughout the year. This is not about eliminating taxes or gaming the system. It is about restoring balance—ensuring that what you owe is planned for, what you earn is usable, and what you keep is intentional.

Throughout this book, one theme has appeared repeatedly: clarity creates calm. When income is visible, when withholding is dynamic, when penalties are prevented before they arise, and when decisions can be tested safely through scenario modeling, fear dissolves. People stop associating growth with risk and success with punishment. Money becomes a tool again rather than a source of stress.

One of the most important insights in this book is that tax stress is rarely about the amount owed. It is about timing, surprise, and loss of control. Owing money is manageable when it is expected. Paying taxes is tolerable when it is proportional and predictable. AI makes this possible by distributing awareness and action across the entire year instead of compressing it into a single moment of reckoning.

Another critical realization is that tax optimization is not a one-time achievement. It is a living system. Income changes. Laws evolve. Life events arrive without warning. Static plans break under these conditions. AI succeeds because it adapts continuously. It does not assume stability. It anticipates movement. This makes tax certainty durable even in an unpredictable world.

As taxes become integrated into everyday financial decision-making, something deeper changes. People begin to act with confidence. They pursue opportunities without hesitation. They invest without fear of hidden consequences.

They plan for the future knowing that taxes are not an invisible threat lurking in the background. This confidence compounds over time, just like money does.

Perhaps the most profound outcome of AI tax forecasting is not financial at all. It is psychological freedom. The quiet removal of stress creates space—space for creativity, ambition, generosity, and enjoyment. When taxes stop interrupting life, life expands.

This book is not the end of a process. It is the foundation of a new way of living financially. One where awareness replaces anxiety, design replaces guesswork, and certainty replaces fear. Artificial intelligence does not remove responsibility—but it removes chaos. And in doing so, it gives people back something far more valuable than money.

It gives them peace.

www.ingramcontent.com/pod-product-compliance
Lightning Source LLC
LaVergne TN
LVHW022024200926
848481LV00007B/2533